Mar'23
Jul'22 11 / 1 / 0

THE AMERICAN REVOLUTION

Lorijo Metz

PowerKiDS
press

New York

Dedicated to Roger Peck, who boldly goes where no historian has gone before!

Published in 2014 by The Rosen Publishing Group, Inc.
29 East 21st Street, New York, NY 10010

First Edition

Editor: Amelie von Zumbusch
Book Design: Colleen Bialecki
Photo Research: Katie Stryker

Photo Credits: Cover Superstock/Getty Images; pp. 5, 9, 11, 12 DEA Picture Library/De Agostini/Getty Images; p. 6 Hulton Archive/Staff/Getty Images; pp. 8, 13, 16 Library of Congress Prints and Photographs Division Washington, D.C.; p. 14 Visions of America/Contributor/Universal Images Group/Getty Images; p. 15 Universal Images Group/Contributor/Getty Images; pp. 13(right), 17, 19 SuperStock/Getty Images; p. 20 Thomas Waterman Wood/The Bridgeman Art Library/Getty Images; p. 21 Mark Krapets/Shutterstock.com; p. 22 Popperfoto/Getty Images.

Library of Congress Cataloging-in-Publication Data

Metz, Lorijo.
  The American Revolution / by Lorijo Metz. — 1st ed.
    pages cm. — (Let's Celebrate Freedom!)
  Includes index.
  ISBN 978-1-4777-2896-3 (library) — ISBN 978-1-4777-2985-4 (pbk.) —
ISBN 978-1-4777-3055-3 (6-pack)
  1. United States—History–Revolution, 1775–1783—Juvenile literature. I. Title.
  E208.M43 2014
  973.3—dc23
                              2013022319

Manufactured in the United States of America

CPSIA Compliance Information: Batch # W14PK4: For Further Information contact Rosen Publishing, New York, New York at 1-800-237-9932

CONTENTS

On July 4, 1776, 13 British **colonies** in North America **declared** their **independence** from Great Britain, one of the most powerful nations in the world. It was a brave act in a time when most people believed only kings could rule large nations. In fact, it was a **revolutionary**, or new and different, action.

The colonists fought a war, now known as the American Revolution, to win their freedom from Great Britain. After they won the war, they went on to create a new country. They even came up with a revolutionary type of government in which the American people would elect their own rulers.

This painting shows the British surrendering after losing the Battles of Saratoga, in New York. The battles were a key win for the Americans and a turning point in the American Revolution.

The events that led to the American Revolution began over 20 years before the first shot rang out. At that point, most people in the 13 colonies were proud to be part of Great Britain, one of the strongest nations in the world. They enjoyed the **protection** that Great Britain gave them. They also enjoyed many freedoms.

Most people in the 13 colonies could trace their families back to Great Britain. This painting shows English settlers arriving at Jamestown, Virginia, in the early seventeenth century.

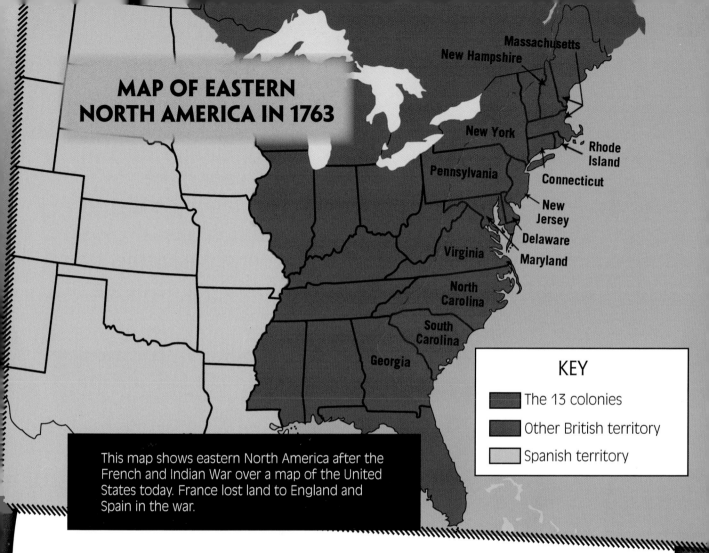

MAP OF EASTERN NORTH AMERICA IN 1763

Massachusetts
New Hampshire
New York
Rhode Island
Connecticut
Pennsylvania
New Jersey
Delaware
Virginia
Maryland
North Carolina
South Carolina
Georgia

KEY
- The 13 colonies
- Other British territory
- Spanish territory

This map shows eastern North America after the French and Indian War over a map of the United States today. France lost land to England and Spain in the war.

Then, the French and Indian War broke out. Between 1754 and 1763, Great Britain fought France for control of North America. Though the British won, the war was costly. To pay for it, the British began taxing the 13 colonies.

The British government, or **Parliament**, passed the Stamp Act in 1765. It taxed colonists on printed materials, such as playing cards and newspapers. The colonists believed the tax was unfair. They had no one to speak for them in Parliament. Though Parliament finally got rid of the Stamp Act, more taxes followed.

Benjamin Franklin printed this cartoon in 1754. It encouraged colonists to unite during the French and Indian War. It became a symbol for the colonies uniting against the British, too.

Tea was one of the colonists' favorite drinks. The Tea Act of 1773 forced colonists to buy tea only from England and pay taxes on it. On December 16, 1773, angry colonists snuck aboard ships and threw 342 chests of tea into Boston Harbor. This event became known as the Boston Tea Party.

Angered by the Boston Tea Party, the British closed Boston Harbor to all trade. They passed new laws, which included sending British officials accused of crimes in the colonies back to England to stand trial. Colonists began to prepare for war.

On April 19, 1775, 700 British soldiers marched into the Massachusetts town of Lexington. They found armed colonists waiting for them. The colonists had been warned that British troops were headed to nearby Concord to seize the colonists' guns and other supplies. No one knows who fired first, but a shot rang out. The American Revolution had begun!

Amos Doolittle made this engraving of the fighting in Lexington in 1775. It was made so that copies could be passed around the colonies to spread news of the battle.

June 15, 1775

The Second Continental Congress makes George Washington the head of the Continental army.

July 4, 1776

The Second Continental Congress adopts the Declaration of Independence.

1771 1772 1773 1774 1775 1776 1777

April 19, 1775

The American Revolution begins with the Battles of Lexington and Concord.

October 19, 1781

General Charles Cornwallis, the leader of the British troops, **surrenders** at Yorktown, Virginia.

1778   1779   1780   1781   1782   1783   1784

October 17, 1777

American troops win the Battles of Saratoga, in New York.

September 3, 1783

Leaders from America, France, Britain, and Spain sign the Treaty of Paris, officially ending the war.

December 26, 1776

Washington wins the Battle of Trenton, in New Jersey.

DECLARING INDEPENDENCE

In May 1775, leaders from across the colonies met to discuss war. At this meeting, called the Second Continental Congress, they appointed George Washington to lead the newly formed Continental army. They also sent King George III of England one last letter asking him to listen to their needs. He ignored them.

John Dunlap printed the first copies of the Declaration of Independence, which were distributed and read throughout the colonies. This is an exact copy of the printing press that he used.

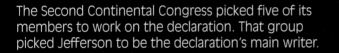

The Second Continental Congress picked five of its members to work on the declaration. That group picked Jefferson to be the declaration's main writer.

On June 7, 1776, Richard Henry Lee of Virginia **proposed** that the colonies should be "free and independent States." While Congress talked about Lee's proposal, Thomas Jefferson began writing an announcement, or declaration. It would explain to the world why the colonies should be free. On July 4, 1776, Congress adopted Jefferson's Declaration of Independence.

FIGHTING THE WAR

By the winter of 1776, the Continental army was losing. Washington had an army of freezing, hungry soldiers. Then, he made a bold move by crossing the Delaware River after nightfall on Christmas Day. Washington's army attacked German soldiers fighting for Britain as they slept in Trenton, New Jersey.

This image shows Washington and his troops crossing the Delaware River from Pennsylvania to New Jersey before the Battle of Trenton.

The British general who surrendered at Yorktown was General Cornwallis. He surrendered to General Washington, as is shown in this image.

It was a key victory, but the war continued. France, Spain, and the Netherlands eventually joined the war on the American side. The final battle took place at Yorktown, Virginia. American and French troops surrounded 7,000 British soldiers, while French ships cut off their escape. The British surrendered on October 19, 1781.

AFTER THE WAR

On September 3, 1783, the United States and Britain signed the Treaty of Paris, officially ending the war. During the war, the 13 colonies declared themselves states. They **united** loosely under the Articles of Confederation. After the war, the articles provided little power for the **federal**, or central, government to pay money it owed to other countries and its own soldiers.

To survive as a nation, the states truly needed to unite. On June 21, 1788, the US **Constitution** became the law of the land. It set up a new government, in which the states and federal government shared power and the people elected their leaders.

American leaders came up with the Constitution at the Constitutional Convention, in Philadelphia. They met in the same building where the Second Continental Congress had met.

INSPIRING A NATION

Leaders of the American Revolution fought for a nation in which "all men are created equal." Unfortunately, many years would pass before the US government would treat everyone equally under the law. However, the idea of the revolution would **inspire** groups such as African Americans and women to fight for equality.

Some states allowed African American men to vote before the Fifteenth Amendment passed. This man is casting his vote in the 1868 election.

The Liberty Bell hung in the building where the Declaration of Independence was signed. It later became a symbol of freedom and a reminder of the American Revolution.

In 1866, the Fourteenth **Amendment** gave Americans of all races equal protection under the law. An amendment is a change to the Constitution. The Fifteenth Amendment, which was passed in 1869, said that African American men must be allowed to vote. In 1920, the Nineteenth Amendment gave women the right to vote.

STILL AN INSPIRATION TODAY

Over 200 years ago, no one could have guessed that a revolution led by 13 colonies would change the world. Shortly after the American Revolution, Poland, France, and several other countries followed the Americans' example and wrote their own constitutions.

The American Revolution continues to inspire in the twenty-first century. Today, more than 190 countries have constitutions that include the idea that all people have basic rights. These echo the rights to "Life, Liberty, and the pursuit of Happiness," listed in our Declaration of Independence.

Figures from the American Revolution, such as George Washington, have become among the best-loved heroes in American history.

GLOSSARY

amendment (uh-MEND-ment) An addition or a change to the Constitution.

colonies (KAH-luh-neez) New places where people move that are still ruled by the leaders of the countries from which they came.

Constitution (kon-stih-TOO-shun) The basic rules by which the United States is governed.

declared (dih-KLAYRD) Officially announced something.

federal (FEH-duh-rul) Having to do with the central government.

independence (in-dih-PEN-dents) Freedom from the control of other people.

inspire (in-SPY-ur) To move someone to do something.

Parliament (PAR-leh-ment) The group in England that makes the country's laws.

proposed (pruh-POHZD) Suggested or planned.

protection (pruh-TEK-shun) Something that keeps something else from being hurt.

revolutionary (reh-vuh-LOO-shuh-ner-ee) New or very different.

surrenders (suh-REN-derz) Gives up.

united (yoo-NYT-ed) Brought together to act as a single group.

INDEX

WEBSITES

Due to the changing nature of Internet links, PowerKids Press has developed an online list of websites related to the subject of this book. This site is updated regularly. Please use this link to access the list: www.powerkidslinks.com/lcf/rev/